COFFIN NAILS & CHRIST

LYNETTE S. DUROCHER

Copyright © 2024 Lynette S. Durocher

All rights reserved.

No portion of this book may be reproduced in any form without written permission from the publisher or author except as permitted by U.S. copyright law.

CONTENTS

INTRODUCTION i
MODERN NAIL SHAPES 1
UNDERSTANDING NAIL SHAPES 3
ROUND 5
SQUARE 7
OVAL 9
ALMOND 11
STILETTO 13
BALLERINA/COFFIN 15
PRACTICAL TIPS AND DIY 17
CONCLUSION 19
GLOSSARY 21
ABOUT THE AUTHOR 1

INTRODUCTION

WHAT IS A HAND today without a manicure? It's still a hand. Exactly.

However, if you take that same hand, moisturize it, and doll it up, then what does it become? It becomes a work of art.

Now, think a step further about what lies inside this hand. It holds provisions and finances. The hand holds promise and opportunity. Lastly, that hand holds potential.

This book is purposed to remind you what you have in your hands.

MODERN NAIL SHAPES

IT IS HARD BEING a woman today. It has always been hard to be a female. Today's modern world will fool people into believing something is true even when it is not. The perception is that we must all look like celebrities every given day and at all times. I say this is unrealistic and that all of us in life have good and bad days. Even those celebrities do not want a camera in their face when they know they don't have make-up on.

Fake nails were a symbol of a woman's status across the world in past times. The symbol was meant to show a woman who did not have to do manual labor.

Well, people, that day has long since been gone for many. I am going to tell you that today, I enjoy getting my nails done professionally. Yes, I can polish and shape my nails. I can groom them neatly and well all by myself. Still, I enjoy treating myself to professionally done nails.

There is something I enjoy about working with my technician to execute the perfect work of art. Although it may only last for one month or some weeks, it is work to be seen and appreciated by others.

As people notice and compliment the work on my hands, I gain a little power on the inside. That power isn't pride; it is confidence.

Those compliments become confidence and create a little more power in me to know I am good enough. A confident woman is a force to reckon with.

UNDERSTANDING NAIL SHAPES

NAIL SHAPES HOLD AN importance today in fashion and self-expression. Design styles tell a story about our individuality. Different people have different styles, and this is good. Variety, in my mind, is intentional of God. If you don't ascribe to this, then tell me, why do we come in so many different races?

Heaven will be made up of many different nations, and that equals races, tribes, peoples, and languages. No matter what, don't let anyone down here on earth stop you from being uniquely you!

Like it is written in the Bible, "For God so loved the world that he gave his only begotten son, that whosoever believe in Him should not perish but have everlasting life." God loves each of us and is unique in His sight.

Let's move on to discuss nail shape terminology. There are many different ways to shape a nail. However, a technician may consider factors such as hand shape, lifestyle, or personal preference before shaping a nail.

Here are some things to consider before picking a nail shape style:

- ❖ Are you small, petite, or young?

- ❖ Are you posh, hardworking, or conservative?
- ❖ Are you a daredevil or dramatic?

Next, let's get into nail shapes.

ROUND

FIRST IS THE ROUND-shaped nail. Most naturalists will love these styles. This style is often for the natural nail girl who is into everyday wear. Her favorite nail color may be simple or classic, like white, cream, or French.

The rounded nail girl believes that all things go 360 degrees. If we are realistic, then we know that at some point in our lives, we will experience a 360-degree moment. A moment where we fell and ended at the same point at which we started something.

Honestly, most people don't want to feel like they have gone around in a circle. Don't believe me? Okay. Get lost in the woods and see what it feels like to go around in 360 degrees, friends.

Sometimes in life, though, a 360-degree experience brings you to a situation with a fresh outlook.

SQUARE

THE NEXT NAIL SHAPE is the Square. The square shape is ideal for a strong, sturdy look and office wear.

While some ladies may enjoy this style, I am not a fan; that's my nail business! In urban terminology, a "square" is known to be a dull, play-it-safe person.

Ladies, I am not here to offend anyone's nail style. What God has for me, it is for me.

That said, I see square shape as a symbol of order. God is a God of decency and order. There is a great degree of power given to the woman who walks in the ordered steps of God. The square-shaped girl is a woman of order and execution, and I love this for her.

OVAL

MOVING ON, WE ARRIVE at the Oval nail shape. This nail shape is ideal for those with elongated fingers. These nail types are chosen by the versatile lady.

I do like and may from time to time donn the oval-shaped nail. I have some long fingers, and versatility is one of my strong suits.

The oval is a symbol of uniqueness and zest for life. Zest is defined as being full of passion, energy, and enthusiasm. If you can't enjoy your new complete set of oval nails for a few weeks, then who can? Power can be coupled with passion, and this lady will become a force with which to reckon.

ALMOND

THE NEXT NAIL SHAPE is Almond.

The almond-shaped nail creates a sense of elegance and has an elongated effect.

Almond nail shapes may require more upkeep, especially due to the pointed tips. The elegant lady is often the same way. She needs more upkeep, and the power that she holds usually has a longer reach.

Hold your skirts, ladies. This won't fly exactly the way that you thought.

God does not look at our outer beauty but our hearts. The elegance that he looks upon is our inner beauty. The woman who feels the power inside her has no problem expressing it on the outside.

Go, almond sisters, go.

STILETTO

NOW, WE MOVE ON to the Stiletto shape.

The Stiletto nail shape is for the bold and dramatic. A good candidate for this style may have shorter fingers. Never fear. Where you lack, sis, God specializes.

Stiletto nails bring out my alter ego. Her name is Stella, and she and I are the same. This nail gives me an inner power that reminds me of an eagle.

An eagle has talons that are sharp and purposeful. They are to capture, subdue, and kill prey. A woman of this power is a substantial force. Her power is captivating; she can put the enemy underneath her feet.

BALLERINA/COFFIN

NOW, WE ARRIVE AT Ballerina/Coffin Nails.

The Coffin nail shape is for the fashionable, high-impact style. This nail shape is my Jam. The shape is known both as Ballerina or Coffin style.

Now, let's get a little deeper into the design of this nail shape.

The nail shape is referred to as Ballerina because of the shape of a ballerina's slipper. The Ballerina is known to stand balancing on her toes in ballet in a form known as toe point— standing on her toes like we stand on God's promises. Surely, a female who can stand on this kind of weight is a power not easily knocked down.

I refer to this shape as coffin nails. It's not the creepy October 31st-type coffin, either.

A coffin is a narrow box of wood in which a corpse is buried. When I get the coffin nail shape, I tend to do "the most."

I would want acrylic nails with gel polish and multiple designs. I would want hand-painted artwork with at least two to three colors on both hands. I tend to add nail jewelry and custom hand art, which easily stand apart from simple one-coat polish nails. Why? It is very simple: my coffin will only be for a short time.

The tomb of Jesus was borrowed from Joseph of Arimathea. Joseph was said to be a wealthy man who believed that Jesus was the Messiah. I believe this man was blessed because he knew Jesus would only need this space for a time.

No, I am not Jesus. Yes, I am his follower. I know that my body one day will die and return to the ground—just my body. Where I am headed will be so much better, brighter, *blingier*. I am a phenomenon and a mystery.

Many times in my life, I was half in that coffin. I was born asthmatic and didn't come home to my parents from the hospital until eight months of age. Then, I contracted Meningitis at 22 from a deli after eating a sandwich. I developed severe Cardiomyopathy at 29 and almost died just a few weeks after having my son. Today, by the grace of God, I am 47 and still here. Not only that, but I plan to remain here for many more years to come.

PRACTICAL TIPS AND DIY

LADIES, DON'T BE FOOLED by these nail shops. They want to use you to make money, of course. You can create the same nail shapes at home by doing it yourself.

Below is a step-by-step guide for creating various nail shapes at home. You will need the following items at home to shape your nails yourself:

- ❖ A sharp nail clipper and a good nail file.
- ❖ A nail buffer. I like the Medium/Coarse gray buffer.
- ❖ Nail drill if you're daring, but it's not necessary.

Nail bits: if you purchase the drill, be careful not to break the cuticle.

- ❖ Gel polishes, and if you are fancy, you can even buy your own UV light friends. I try not to use UV light too often, as we want to avoid any issues down the line with exposure.

CONCLUSION

THIS HAS BEEN A public service announcement for our hands and our hearts.

Ladies, you can take matters into your own hands and do your nails yourself. Doing your nails takes no power that was given to you away from you. You are a woman, and your feminine power will always exist whether you decide to go with plain nails and clear polish or go all the way out and accessorize with the works.

You will always be powerful.

Now that you know what I have been through, leave me in my lane when I am rocking my coffin-shaped nails. Leave these ladies alone and let them choose whatever style they identify with. Power lies within each one. Mind your business on the weeks or months we don't get our nails done.

What lies in your hands isn't just the tapping on a surface with our fake nails. The true thing that lies in our hands is our power, which comes from God.

GLOSSARY

1. The Holy BIBLE: John 3:16, For God so loved the world, that he gave his only begotten Son, that whosoever believeth in him should not perish, but have everlasting life.
2. Tabitha Brown: "And that's your Business"
3. The Holy BIBLE: 1 Corinthians 14:40, Let all things be done decently and in order.
4. The Holy BIBLE: Psalms 34:12(MSG): "Who out there has a zest for life? Can't wait each day to come upon beauty."
5. The Holy Bible: Matthew 27:57-58, "As evening approached there came a rich man from Arimathea, named Joseph, who had himself become a disciple of Jesus. Going to Pilate, he asked for Jesus' body, and Pilate ordered that it be given to him.
6. https://federico.edu>theultimate At_Home Guide to Shaping Your Nails Like A Pro.

ABOUT THE AUTHOR

LYNETTE S. DUROCHER is a businessperson, author, healthcare worker, and social media content creator.

Lynette is a mom to two children, Trin and E.J., and they live together in Florida.

Alongside her husband, Ro, they founded Stella Ro, LLC. They have developed this business to save lost souls and encourage and build faith in Christians and non-believers. They have two active brands, including Brown Sugar for classic car enthusiasts and Smack Talk and Abide for Christian streetwear, and soon to include novels, ready-to-wear clothing, and Kitchenware.

"As for my house and me," Lynette often quotes, "we will abide in the secret place of the Most High God."

Hope to see you soon!

www.ingramcontent.com/pod-product-compliance
Lightning Source LLC
Chambersburg PA
CBHW060623070426
42449CB00042B/2478